How GOOD
is good enough?

LifeChange Books

ANDY STANLEY

Multnomah® Publishers *Sisters, Oregon*

HOW GOOD IS GOOD ENOUGH?
published by Multnomah Publishers, Inc.

© 2003 by Andy Stanley
International Standard Book Number: 1-59052-274-5
International Standard Book Number: 1-59052-359-8 (pb)

Image © Tom Collicott/Graphistock

Unless otherwise indicated, Scripture quotations are from:
The Holy Bible, New International Version © 1973, 1984
by International Bible Society, used by permission of
Zondervan Publishing House.

Multnomah is a trademark of Multnomah Publishers, Inc.,
and is registered in the U.S. Patent and Trademark Office.
The colophon is a trademark of Multnomah Publishers, Inc.

Printed in the United States of America

For information:
MULTNOMAH PUBLISHERS, INC. • P.O. BOX 1720 • SISTERS, OR 97759

Library of Congress Cataloging-in-Publication Data
Stanley, Andy.
    How good is good enough? / by Andy Stanley.
        p. cm.
Includes bibliographical references (p. 93).
    ISBN 1-59052-359-8
    1. Christian life. 2. Conduct of life. 3. Heaven. I. Title.
BV4501.3.S732 2003
234—dc21
                        2003012465

03 04 05 06 07 08—10 9 8 7 6 5 4

To Helen Waldrep

CONTENTS

PART I

How Do You Get
There from Here?

The story is told of a Sunday school teacher whose assignment was to explain to the six-year-olds in his class what someone had to do in order to go to heaven. In an attempt to discover what the kids already believed about the subject, he asked a few questions.

"If I sold my house and my car, had a big garage sale, and gave all my money to the church, would that get me into heaven?"

"NO!" the children all answered.

"If I cleaned the church every day, mowed the yard, and kept everything neat and tidy, would *that* get me into heaven?"

Again the answer was, "NO!"

"Well then," he said, "if I was kind to animals and gave candy to all the children and loved my wife, would that get me into heaven?"

Again they all shouted, "NO!"

"Well then, how *can* I get into heaven?"

A boy in the back row stood up and shouted, "YOU GOTTA BE DEAD!"

DEAD SURE

Therein lies the problem: You gotta be dead to go to heaven. Consequently, you gotta be dead to know much about the place, as well.

The people who seem to be most confident about what heaven is like are those who claim to have died and come back to talk about it—and write bestselling books on the subject. I have read a couple of those books, and I've heard a couple of "returners" interviewed on television. Their stories are interesting. But they never give a straight answer to the questions we are all asking: "How do you get there? What can we do on this side of death to assure ourselves a spot in heaven?"

Most agree that death is a prerequisite, but that's pretty much where agreement ends and speculation begins. In these pages, we are going to look at an ancient but popular theory regarding who goes to heaven. I say ancient, because the idea has been around since the beginning of civilization. In terms of popularity, it is what most world religions espouse.

So why did I bother to write a book about it? Because in spite of its immense popularity and long standing, it doesn't make a lick of sense.

Seriously. Smart, educated, accomplished men and women from just about every nation on earth are banking their eternities on a theory that doesn't hold up under even the slightest scrutiny.

Why? Well, I'm not sure. My assumption is that everybody is preoccupied with making a living, falling in love, having kids, and whatever else they are doing. Nobody's got time to think about heaven. So they don't.

THE GREAT EQUALIZER

But every now and again we are confronted with our mortality. When that happens, we mentally take hold of *something* that gives us assurance. For most people on this spinning ball of minerals and dirt, assurance is found in an assumption they have never tested. And it brings them the assurance they need to jump right back into the game of life.

So what is this internationally held assumption?

Good people go to heaven.

The logic flows something like this: There is a good God who lives in a good place reserved for good people. This God goes by many names. He is behind all major world religions. Therefore, all major, and possibly minor, religions provide a legitimate path to God and, therefore, heaven. The criterion for making it to this good place is to be good. Each religion has its own definition for *good*. But what they all have in common is that men and women must do certain things, and not do certain things, in order to assure themselves a spot in this good place with a good God.

Make sense?

Actually, it doesn't really make any sense at all. In fact, if you are smart enough to read this book, you are smart enough to find the problems with the *good people go* view without my help. Chances are, you've never really thought it through. But you owe it to yourself to do so.

I figure it will take you about two hours to read this book. Investing two hours of your time to consider where you will spend eternity isn't really much to ask. So find a comfortable chair and prepare yourself for what may be an uncomfortable discovery.

Chapter 1

EVERYTHING'S FINE

If you are like most people, you believe that everybody lives forever somewhere, that once you die, your soul goes somewhere. Most Americans believe in heaven. A smaller percentage believe in hell. In other parts of the world, the prevailing belief is that the soul comes back around for another lap—we just start over as someone (or something) else.

In spite of all their differences and peculiarities, the religions of this world share one common denominator: How you live your life on this side of the grave determines what happens next. Western thought has all the good people going to heaven. In other parts of the world, the good people come back around as even better people, or at least with the opportunity to become better people.

THINK ABOUT IT

Here's something to think about: If God appeared to you and asked, "Why should I let you into heaven?" how would you answer? If you're like most people, your answer might run something along these lines:

"I've always tried to…"

"I never…"

"I do my best…"

Whether I am talking to Muslims, Hindus, or Christians, the majority of the answers I receive to that question go back to an individual's attempt to live a good life. Why? Because most people believe that good people go to heaven.

The moral? Behave yourself now and you don't really need to worry too much about what happens next. The end. Now let's get back to work, golf, Little League, PTA—the pressing issues of this life.

PACKED AND READY

But then every once in a while something happens that forces you to seriously consider the question of what's next—a funeral, a health scare, a birthday, a glance in the mirror. You don't like to think about it. You rarely ever talk about it. But it is always there. And the older you get, the more often you find yourself pushing it from your mind.

The fact is, the mortality rate for humans is 100 percent. And that bothers you. In spite of the fact that you believe there *is* something better on the other side of life, you are not at peace. And for good reason.

You see, as good as you are—and you are pretty good—you aren't *really* sure if you have been good enough. You hope so. And you are certainly better than…well…than certain people you know.

But how good is good enough?

Where's the line? Who is the standard? Where do you currently stand? Do you have enough time left to stash away enough good deeds to counterbalance your bad ones?

And while we're asking questions, I'll go ahead and throw one in that perhaps you've wondered about but were afraid to ask: Just *who* is in charge of this operation? God? If so, he ought to have been a bit clearer about how this whole thing works. If our eternal residence hangs in the balance based on how we live, we could certainly do with some direction. A standard. A mile marker or two. Perhaps a midterm.

"But wait," you say, "isn't it the job of religion to answer those questions for me?" Sure. Most of the various world religions and their books do exist to answer those questions. Teachers, preachers, ulema, rabbis, priests, lamas—they are all in the business of getting us safely to the other side. Specifically, they are responsible for helping you and me understand how to live in such a way as to ensure a happy ending.

So why are you still unsure? You've been to church. Perhaps you attended a few religion classes as a child. And yet, if you are like the majority of people I talk to, you still are not confident where you stand with God.

I ran across an interesting quote by Gandhi that underscored the universal uncertainty associated with religious belief. When questioned why he proselytized in the arena of politics but not religion, he responded, "In the realm of the political and social and economic, we can be sufficiently certain to convert; but in the realm of religion there is not sufficient certainty to convert anybody, and, therefore, there can be no conversions in religions."[1] Now that's helpful, isn't it? Even Gandhi didn't find certainty in religion.

TO GRANDMOTHER'S HOUSE WE GO

Several years ago my wife, Sandra, walked into our kitchen, sat down on the bar stool, and announced that she wanted to make a special trip to her hometown for the expressed purpose of talking to her aging grandmother, Helen, about eternity. I was surprised. Helen was almost ninety at the time. She grew up going to the local Methodist church. Until her health became an issue, she rarely missed a Sunday. She was way better than the average person. Certainly *good* by anybody's standard.

"What brought this on?" I asked.

"I'm not sure," Sandra said. "I just don't know how much longer she will be with us, and I've never talked to her about God or heaven or any of that." For most people who knew Helen, her ultimate destination would be the least of their concerns. If good people go to heaven, she was a shoo-in. Nevertheless, Sandra hopped in the car and drove two and a half hours to chat with her grandmother.

Helen knew she was coming. Sandra showed up under the guise of wanting to make cookies. But after about thirty minutes of chitchat, she popped the question. She said, "Grandmama, we've never talked about heaven before. Are you sure that when you die you will go to heaven?"

Helen got big tears in her eyes and responded the way the average *good* person responds to that question. She said, "I hope so, honey."

"I hope so"? Ninety years of good living, standing by her dying husband till the end, serving her community, loving her grandchildren, paying her taxes, driving the speed limit, and she *hopes* she's going to heaven? If Helen can't go to sleep at night with the peace of knowing that things between her and her creator are good, I'm not sure who can. If Helen ain't sure, can't nobody be sure.

So why is it that even the *really good* people at best "hope so"? I'll tell you why. Because nobody can tell you how good you have to be to go to heaven.

Nobody.

Don't believe me? Get out the phone book and start calling the religious leaders in your community. You will get an earful of information, but when the words finally quit flowing, you'll be back to "I hope so."

Chapter 2

A Dangerous
Assumption

One thing I don't worry about is waking up to a smoke-filled bedroom with little or no time to escape. You want to know why? Because I have four smoke alarms. That's right, *four!* I am *so* safe. You know what else I have? Two fire extinguishers. One in the kitchen and one in our master bedroom. Between our smoke alarms and our fire extinguishers, we have nothing to worry about when it comes to fire. We are safe. Unless, of course, our builder forgot to put batteries in the smoke detectors. If that's the case, we might as well have a couple of Frisbees attached to our ceilings.

By the way, when is the last time you tested your smoke detectors? I've never tested mine. I stare at them occasionally and wonder why the installer didn't line them up with the recessed lighting. But I don't know if they actually work. The company that installed my burglar alarm told me that my smoke detectors were wired into the alarm system. I nodded like I understood what he was talking about. I've often wondered why they did that. I guess if a burglar breaks in and the smoke detectors go off, the burglar is fooled into thinking the house is on fire. Or something like that.

And about those fire extinguishers: For all I know, they are full of shaving cream. A friend of mine told me I should test my fire extinguishers. He's probably right. But I've never gone to the trouble. Sounds messy to me. Yet in spite of my lack of investigation, I go to bed every night under the assumption that my family and I are safe from fire.

Likewise, most of the world goes to bed at night under the assumption that if they were to die in their sleep, they would find themselves standing at the pearly gates. After all, good people go to heaven. And just about everybody thinks they are good.

UNTESTED ASSUMPTIONS

I have never met anyone who spent even a minimal amount of time testing the assumption that good people go to heaven. And I can understand why. Most of us are just way too busy to sit around trying to unravel the mysteries of the universe. But more to the point, it just makes sense that good people would go to heaven.

The logic behind *good people go to heaven* is seemingly impenetrable on two accounts. First, it is fair. By fair, I mean people who do good deserve good things. If you do well in school, you move to the next grade. If you do well in tryouts, you make the team. If you do well on the job, you receive raises and promotions. Being rewarded for your efforts is part of our human experience and expectation, so it makes sense that this dynamic originated with God. After all, this cause-and-effect relationship is illustrated in all mainstream religious literature. The Bible, the Koran, and the Book of Mormon all recount God's eagerness to reward good behavior in this life. So it only seems fair that if you do well in this life, you should go to heaven.

Second, it coincides with the notion that there is a good God. If there is a good God, and if he dwells in a good place, then it makes sense that God would fill heaven with good people. If heaven were full of "bad" people, it wouldn't be heaven. A good God in a good place sounds like the ideal destination for good people.

EVERYBODY WINS

Besides the fact that this view appeals to our common sense, it is good for society. It keeps everybody on their best behavior—or at least it should. If only the good people go, you had better be good! Offer a trip to Walt Disney World as incentive for good behavior, and even the most troublesome of kids can muster the self-control needed to earn their ears. If you believe heaven hangs in the balance, hinging on whether or not you do good, chances are you are going to do good.

But the best thing about this way of thinking is that it guarantees you a place in heaven. You make the cut, right? You are good enough to go to heaven. I know, I know. You are not perfect. For most of us, that's an unnecessary disclaimer—nobody has ever accused me of being perfect. But at the same time, you feel as if you are close enough to make it to heaven.

Or maybe you don't think you make the cut. Maybe you picked up this book because you believe good people go to heaven and you're not one of them. If that's the case, you may want to move on to the next chapter. But the truth is, very few people who believe in life after death feel as though they aren't going to a good place.

In a recent survey, people were asked if they believed in heaven and hell. Almost 90 percent of Americans said they believed there is a heaven, while only 30 percent believed in hell as a real place. And almost nobody who believed in hell thought they were going there. In that case, maybe we should retire to the dining room for drinks and dinner. It would seem we are all out of danger. Good people go to heaven, and any view to the contrary is indefensible.

What other view could there possibly be? Perhaps *bad people go to heaven?* Unthinkable! Every major world religion subscribes to the notion that our deeds here on earth determine our destination in the afterlife. *All* the experts can't be wrong. Can they?

Chapter 3

"God Is Great, God Is Good"

God may be good, but life isn't always good. In fact, life is the primary reason people struggle with the notion of a good God.

If God is good, why_____?

You can fill in the blank for yourself. If God is powerful enough to get the good people to heaven, then why can't he take better care of us on earth?

No doubt you have heard someone ask this question before. Probably asked it yourself on occasion. I've got another one for you. Ready?

If God is so good, why didn't he do a better job of declaring his expectations for us so that we don't have to live our whole lives wondering where we stand?

If good people go to heaven, a good God should have communicated that directly to us. Instead, we have religious leaders of all shapes, sizes, and persuasions who claim that they know the formula. The problem, of course, is that they all have a different formula.

At this point there's always a temptation to oversimplify and say something like, "Well, all religions are basically the same." Basically, maybe. But once you tune in to the specifics, they are miles apart. Even within single disciplines there isn't agreement. Read the history of Islam. Compare the messages you hear in a Catholic church to what the Baptists are saying. Compare the teachings of Jewish rabbis in the Middle Ages to what they are saying now. When it comes to specifics, religion is all over the map. And as open-minded as I try to be, everybody *can't* be right.

Why such disparity in teachings? Because your suspicions are correct. Most originated with a bunch of men who claim to have heard from God and are now called to tell the rest of us what he wants us to do and how he wants us to live.

In recent days, we have all become uncomfortably familiar with certain groups of religious zealots who are convinced that blowing people up is good and that it secures for them a place in paradise. I think they are seriously deceived. But who am I to judge? They are simply following the teachings of their religious leaders. That's what most of us do, isn't it? The difference? Application. You believe God wants you to love your neighbors; they believe God wants them to blow up their neighbors.

Is their God good? They think so.

Is your God good? You probably think so.

But if being good—the way I measure *good*—will get me into heaven, the terrorists won't be there. At least, not in my neighborhood.

GOOD GOD, BAD GOD

You see, once you get past the emotional appeal, the *good people go* view has some major problems.

First of all, if good people go to heaven, then we need a clear and consistent definition for what is good. We need a list. We need to know that the rules reflect God's standard, not something manufactured by important-looking guys in robes.

If God allows good people into heaven, but he does not bother to specify what he means by *good*, it leaves me to wonder just how good God is. Let me illustrate.

Pretend for a moment that you have signed up to participate in a race. You're standing at the starting line with all the other runners. Up ahead you notice that the road forks off in three directions. You also note the total absence of signs, flags, or markers. You ask a race official for a map and are informed that there is no map. And your eyes haven't deceived you; there are no markers of any kind signifying the boundaries of the course. "What is the distance?" you ask. The race official just shrugs his shoulders and replies, "You just run. We will tell you when you cross the finish line, assuming you find it." With no warning, the starting gun is fired and the runners take off in half a dozen different directions.

Would you call that a good race? Would you sign up for next year's event? Would you recommend this race to a friend?

Consider this. It's the first day of school, and your professor informs you that your class grade will be based entirely on how well you do on the final exam. She then announces that class is dismissed and there will be no further class meetings until the end of the term. Panicked, you throw up your hand and ask, "Is there a syllabus or reading list? Are you going to assign a textbook?"

The professor smiles and says, "None of that is necessary. Just be ready for the final." And out she goes. Good teacher? A class you would recommend?

No Application Necessary

Unrealistic? Sure. But let's be honest. If there is life beyond this one, and where you end up is determined by your "test score" here, do you really have anything specific to go on? "Be good" is about as helpful as "run fast."

Run where?

If there is a level of performance that will get us into heaven and God neglects to tell us exactly what it is, can we with good conscience call him good? If so, then *good* takes on a completely different meaning. Good no longer means fair and just. It means…well…we don't really know what it means, do we?

But it gets worse.

If there is a level of performance that gets us into heaven and God neglects to tell us exactly what it is, then you are not only good, you are better than God! That's right. Think about it. *You* would never hold people you cared about to a standard you refused to reveal.

As an employer, you wouldn't withhold a job description from your employees and then evaluate them by a standard they never had an opportunity to see. As a teacher, you wouldn't give tests on material you never covered. When mere mortals act in this manner, we complain vehemently. We yank our kids out of those schools. We refuse to work for those kinds of companies. We expect more from our fellow man. Yet when it comes to God, somehow we have grown accustomed to his duplicity. Apparently, the whole world has.

THE TRUTH IS IN US

"But wait," you say, "maybe God *has* given us a standard. Isn't there a built-in sense of right and wrong inside all of us? Doesn't everybody know that it's wrong to steal, kill, lie, and break the speed limit?" Okay, maybe we had better stick with steal, kill, and lie. And the answer is yes. At least for the most part. And I am inclined to agree that this general sense of morality that resides in humanity has its source in God. Where else could it have come from?

If we just made it up, it is awfully difficult to explain how people of every nation throughout recorded history have continued to arrive at similar conclusions regarding right and wrong, fair and unfair. There sure seems to be a source for these standards outside of individual tastes and preferences.

Evidence for the divine origin of this universal ethic is the fact that we continually violate it. I believe it is wrong to break the law, but I repeatedly break the speed limit. Why would I believe something is morally binding that I have little inclination to follow? Strange, isn't it?

It is as if two forces are at work in me (and you). To complicate matters further, when people speed through my neighborhood, potentially endangering the lives of my kids, I get really mad. Mad about something I am guilty of doing myself.

So what about this internal sense of right and wrong? Is it enough to guide you toward a lifestyle that earns for you a place in heaven or perhaps another trip through life at an elevated status?

Chapter 4

MORE INPUT
NEEDED

Your conscience is an interesting thing. It condemns you when you do bad, but it doesn't do much in the way of assuring you when you do well. It reminds you that you aren't perfect, but it gives you no direction in terms of how perfect you need to be to secure a reservation on the other side.

That's where religion takes over. Your inner sense of right and wrong reminds you that you have a ways to go. Religious experts grab the baton at that point and try to help you understand the specifics required to earn your way into heaven.

Think about it. If your inner sense of right and

wrong had the ability to reassure you when things were right between you and God, there would be no need for religion at all. We would all know exactly where we stand. You wouldn't need other men and women telling you what you should and should not do; it would be intuitive. And there would be agreement across cultural and generational lines regarding what is right and wrong. But as you know, once you move beyond "Thou shalt not kill, lie, and steal," diversity of opinion abounds.

In the seventeenth century, Giordano Bruno, a disciple of famed astronomer Nicolaus Copernicus, had the audacity to suggest that space was boundless and that the sun and its planets were but one of any number of similar systems.

What was he thinking?

Bruno was condemned by the church, tried before the Inquisition, and burned at the stake. The *church?* The church burned somebody at the stake for believing the earth wasn't the center of the universe? Was that right? Was that good? They thought so. I don't. Do you?

Famed astronomer Galileo was brought forward in 1633 on similar charges. Under the threat of torture and death, he was forced to renounce all belief in Copernican theories. He was then sentenced to house arrest for the remainder of his days.

Wait a minute. Religious leaders ought to know better. They are appointed by God. Or maybe they just volunteered.... Anyway, they are the ones who are supposed to help the rest of us understand how to win our way to heaven.

In recent days we have learned details of the persecution of women in religious Taliban-controlled communities, where an unveiled face could result in a beating. That seems unjust to me, but apparently not to them. In my view, I think any man who beats a woman ought to be.... Well, you might not finish the book if I told you what I thought about men who hurt women. Suffice it to say that I view God and good differently than they do. One of us is wrong.

But if God has placed in each of our hearts a universal sense of right and wrong that serves as our guide for working our way to heaven...well, I'm confused.

It's hard to find two people, much less two cultures, that are on the same page regarding what good *is,* much less *how* good we must be to make it to heaven. I read a book years ago about an anthropologist who spent time with a New Guinea tribe that celebrated betrayal. The ability to win the confidence of someone in order to later betray him was viewed as a virtue. In fact, when Christian missionaries presented the story of Jesus, tribal members stood up and clapped when the storyteller got to the part about Judas betraying Christ. They thought Judas was the hero of the story!

The point being, there is no true consensus of conscience among humanity. I know what feels right to me, and I would love it if the whole world would adopt my personal value system and act accordingly. And yet I keep running into folks who insist on operating according to the way *they* see things.

THINGS CHANGE

Another problem with trusting in our internal sense of right and wrong to act as a divine compass is that our perception of right and wrong changes as time passes. Have you noticed that? What I was dogmatic about in my twenties doesn't seem to matter as much in my forties.

I ran into a friend from high school, Katie, whom I hadn't seen in twenty years. Last time our paths crossed she was moving up north to live with her boyfriend. Seemed the right thing to do, at the time. Twenty years later, Katie looked at me with tears in her eyes and said it was the biggest mistake of her life. She even used the *S* word—she said her decision was a *sin*. Katie is determined to instill a different value system in her fourteen-year-old daughter.

Was moving in with her boyfriend a sin? At twenty-one, she didn't think so. At forty-two, Katie sees things differently. So which is it? If there is an internal sense of right and wrong that is divinely instilled in each of us, and it is complete enough to get us to heaven, why does it change through the years? If Katie had been killed in a car accident at twenty-three, would she have gone to heaven? I don't know. She doesn't think so.

The church I grew up in has an embarrassing civil rights history. In the early fifties, black people were absolutely not welcomed there. I read in the church archives of an incident that was so unbelievable to me that I tracked down somebody who attended during those years to verify it. Sure enough, one Sunday morning a black woman arrived early for a Sunday morning service. She sat in the third row on the aisle. There were only a few other people in the sanctuary at the time. One by one they got up and left. Soon a crowd gathered in the narthex. The deacons wouldn't allow anyone to enter until they could figure out what to do. After a brief meeting they decided to turn off the lights! Can you imagine?

Now here's the interesting thing: I am certain they believed in their hearts that they were doing the right thing.

When the black woman still didn't leave, two deacons went in and asked her to leave the premises. She agreed. Once the *crisis* had passed, everyone filed into the sanctuary and the worship service began. As the pastor and music director took their places on the platform, the congregation stood to their feet and sang:

> Praise God, from whom all blessings flow.
>   Praise Him, all creatures here below.
> Praise Him above, ye heavenly host.
>   Praise Father, Son, and Holy Ghost.
> Aaaaaaaaaa-men!

These were men and women who claimed to love God. But surely their values didn't reflect God's? Or did they? I don't think so. You probably don't either.

I mentioned that I talked to a lady who was present that day. She said that years later, many from that congregation confessed that they were ashamed of the way they had acted that day. As the world changed around them, they saw how wrong they had been. What they viewed as an effort to protect their church during one season of their lives was later viewed as pure racism.

My point? We change. And as we change, our values, morals, and ethics change. So which standard does God use? Our adolescent standard? Our single-and-free standard? Our married-with-children standard? Our too-old-to-care standard? Or does he have his own set of rules that he just hasn't bothered to share with us?

OBJECTION!

I live in the Bible belt. And right about now, readers in the Bible belt are asking, "What about the Bible? What about the Ten Commandments? Didn't God give us the Bible to show us how to live?"

Some people think so.

Chapter 5

DIDN'T MO' KNOW?

While I was in graduate school in Dallas, I lived in a pretty rough area of the city. Walking distance from my efficiency apartment, there was a dry cleaner managed by a wonderful old lady named Phyllis. From time to time I was able to engage Phyllis in conversations that went beyond the recent exploits of the Cowboys or the Rangers. On one occasion, I mentioned how I often felt unsafe in my own neighborhood. One thing led to another, and before long we were talking about death and heaven and angels and all kinds of stuff that neither of us knew much about. As I was leaving, Phyllis made a final comment that caused me to stop and turn around. "If something were to happen to me," she said, "I know I would go to heaven."

"Really?" I said. "Why's that?"

"Because I keep the Ten Commandments," she said.

That struck me as strange. "Phyllis, do you even *know* the Ten Commandments?"

She smiled and sheepishly admitted that she knew a few of them.

"Do you know where in the Bible the Ten Commandments are found?" I asked.

"Nope," she said, "but I sure as hell don't break any of 'em!"

LOOK FOR YOURSELF

Phyllis knew there were some laws somewhere in the Bible. And she assumed, as many do, that there is some connection between those laws and where a person spends eternity.

But the fact is, there is no connection between the Ten Commandments and heaven. None. Nada. Zero. It doesn't exist. You don't have to take my word for it; you can pick up a Bible and check it out for yourself.

The Ten Commandments are found in the book of Exodus. Interesting book. But there is no promise of heaven for people who keep the Ten Commandments. There is no mention anywhere in Exodus of the afterlife or eternal bliss. In fact, the dearth of writings by Moses pertaining to the afterlife led at least one powerful segment of Jewish religious leaders, the Sadducees, to not believe in the afterlife at all!

These Jewish scholars, men who spent their entire lives studying the Scriptures, arrived at the conclusion that keeping the Ten Commandments in no way guaranteed a person anything beyond this life. And this is the same list of do's and don'ts that many are depending upon to get them to heaven.

THE LIST GOES ON

If you read the entire book of Exodus, you will discover that there aren't just ten commandments; there are dozens of commandments, most of which none of us have kept. And not only are there lots of commandments, but many come with specific consequences attached. In Exodus 21:17, just a few verses removed from God's Top Ten, it says, "Anyone who curses his father or mother must be put to death."

A bit extreme for my taste. But if you are really serious about hanging your eternity on your ability to keep the Old Testament commandments, you've got to adopt the whole system, not just the parts that are convenient. "Thou shalt not murder" doesn't threaten my lifestyle too much, but "Thou shalt not covet thy neighbor's house" hits a little closer to home. Especially if that includes furnishings.

My point? Don't look to the Bible, certainly not the Old Testament, for a list of things to do to ensure your place in heaven. The standard is too high. Besides, you have to sacrifice a bull or cow or pigeon to get right with God every time you break a commandment. The Ten Commandments are part of a complicated system of laws and sacrifices. Trust me, you don't have the time— or the facilities—to embrace everything necessary to approach God that way.

So if the Ten Commandments weren't given as a means of earning our way to heaven, what was their purpose?

WHAT'S THE POINT?

The Old Testament law was given primarily to provide a social and civil framework for the nation of Israel. Just as we have laws that govern our society, so Israel needed laws to live by.

When Moses showed up, the Israelites had been enslaved in Egypt for four hundred years. They had no laws or system of government. Slaves don't need that sort of thing. Once they were free from Egypt, all of that changed. So God gave his people a system of rules to live by that were in keeping with the way he thought people should conduct themselves. But nowhere did he promise heaven for those who kept the law. And nowhere did he threaten hell for those who didn't. In fact, God didn't expect Israel to keep the law perfectly. That's why he prescribed the elaborate system of sacrifices.

On several occasions, the people of Israel ignored God's law and adopted the laws of surrounding nations. When Israel got off track, God sent prophets to warn the people. But even when Israel chose to ignore God's warnings, never did he threaten to abandon his people or send them to hell.

Again, there seem to be no eternal ramifications to keeping or breaking God's law. Consequences? Yes, but never the promise of heaven or the threat of hell.

FALLING DOWN

Unlike the Old Testament, which seemingly ignores issues of eternity, the New Testament is full of stuff about heaven and hell. But once again, we find no help in our quest for a standard by which we can earn favor with God. Here's what the New Testament says about working our way into heaven:

> All have sinned and fall short of the glory of God.
>
> ROMANS 3:23

> There is no one righteous, not even one.
> ROMANS 3:10

> For the wages of sin is death.
> ROMANS 6:23

And check this one out:

> Therefore no one will be declared righteous in
> [God's] sight by observing the law; rather,
> through the law we become conscious of sin.
> ROMANS 3:20

The New Testament comes right out and says what the Old Testament implies: *No one will reach God by being good.*

I'm not arguing that the Bible is correct; I'm just pointing out that the Bible offers no help in our quest to find a magic list. Not only does the Bible not offer any help, it discourages us from even looking.

Chapter 6

GRADING ON
THE CURVE

Earlier I said that the *good people go* view has several
hurdles to clear. The first is that there is no universal consensus regarding what is right and what is wrong. The
second follows from the first.

Assume for a moment that you *do* know, and agree
with, a definition of right and wrong. Assume you somehow know in divinely certain terms what constitutes *good*.
Even if that were the case, you are still left with the
quandary of how you are to be graded and where you stand
at any given time. When you die, do you get to go to
heaven if your good deeds constitute 70 percent of your
overall deeds? Or does 51 percent earn you a passing grade?

I'm not trying to be silly. If you believe good people go to heaven, then this is a relevant question. What percentage of your deeds do you think need to be allotted to the positive side of the balance sheet in order to secure a slot in heaven? Come on. Play along. Make a guess. Never thought about it? Have no idea? Neither do I. That's because God has not revealed it to you or me.

But let's take it one step further. Let's assume that God is extraordinarily merciful and that only 10 percent of your deeds need to be good to get you into heaven. Even then, you could find yourself one good work shy of a passing grade. Imagine that! You miss out on heaven because you're short one lousy act of kindness. To make matters worse, you had no idea the difference one act of kindness would make because God never bothered to make the system clear.

Or what if God's holiness and perfection outweigh his mercy and he requires that 90 percent of our deeds be good? Or what if God grades on a curve and Mother Teresa skewed the cosmic curve, raising the bar for good deeds beyond what most of us are capable of? Granted, heaven would be sparsely populated, but who knows? When she was around, Mother Teresa was constantly calling men and women out of their comfort zones to follow in her commitment to love the poor and downtrodden. Maybe God was speaking to us through her. Maybe she knew something most of us have missed. Again, we don't know.

While we are in *what if* mode, consider this: Under the *good people go* scenario, you could simply run out of time. Think about it. Right now, it could be that you do not have enough time to do the good deeds necessary to make up for your bad ones. You could be condemned to whatever else is out there right this minute and not know it.

"Surely not," you argue. You hope not. But you don't know. I don't know. Your pastor doesn't know. Only God knows how much time you have left, and he's holding his cards close to his vest.

IF I WERE GOD

If God is good and good people go to heaven, shouldn't God show up every generation or so and give us the updated version of what he expects? Goodness 7.0. Why make us dependent on prophets and teachers who have been dead for a thousand years or more? Has God lost his voice?

In spite of his deafening silence on the subject, the majority of us cling to the hope that good people go to heaven and we are the good ones. Granted, it is comforting to imagine a God who values our strengths and pretty much ignores our weaknesses. But that is the God of our imaginations, not necessarily the God who exists.

Do you know why the various world religions cling to this view in one form or another? Because there aren't any good options. What else can we believe? If good people don't go, who does?

Perhaps everybody goes to heaven. That would be great. But that would mean the majority of religious leaders have misled us for generations. And if everybody is going to make it, why doesn't God just tell us?

LAST BUT NOT LEAST

Next we will examine a third and perhaps the most surprising obstacle to the *good people go* view. You may be tempted to close the book at some point in this next chapter. But since you have waded in this far, you owe it to yourself to push on. For as we are about to discover, there was one major religious figure who did not believe that good people go to heaven.

Chapter 7

LIAR, LIAR

Perhaps the most emotionally perplexing problem with the *good people go to heaven* view is that it contradicts the teachings of Jesus Christ. In fact, if good people go to heaven, Jesus completely misled his audiences and, on at least one occasion, wrongly comforted a dying man. The truth is, Jesus taught the very opposite of what most people in the world believe.

Jesus taught that good people *don't* go to heaven.

Furthermore, he taught that God was intent on not giving people what they deserved. Jesus claimed that God desires to give men and women exactly what they do *not* deserve.

Not only was this a major departure from the religious teachings of his day, it was a departure from anything that had ever been taught anywhere at any time by anyone. The whole idea was so unsettling that Jewish religious leaders had the man arrested and crucified. After all, you can't have someone running around saying that God loves bad people and that bad people go to heaven. That might result in a moral free-for-all!

RAISING THE ANTE

Jesus did a few other things that infuriated leaders of the religious establishment. For starters, he declared that even the best among them was not good enough to reach God on his own merit.

> For I tell you that unless your righteousness sur-
> passes that of the Pharisees and the teachers of
> the law, you will certainly not enter the kingdom
> of heaven.
>
> MATTHEW 5:20

When it came to keeping the law, the Pharisees were the best people around. Remember the complicated Old Testament laws we discussed earlier? The Pharisees actually tried to *do* all that stuff. It was their job. They were professional do-gooders. Their job was to stay so pure before God that they would be able to hear from him and thus direct the people accordingly.

They took their job seriously. Not only did they keep the law that was given by Moses, they came up with even more rules to ensure that they didn't accidentally break one of Moses' rules. I'm not exaggerating when I say that these men spent the majority of their time making sure they were the best of the best.

So you can imagine how irritated they were when Jesus pointed to several of them in public and announced that unless a person's goodness surpassed that of the finest men in town, that person wouldn't make it into God's kingdom. Basically, he pointed to the Pharisees and said, "As good as you are, you aren't good enough."

While the Pharisees walked away mad, everybody else probably walked away depressed. After all, if their religious leaders weren't good enough, then who could be? The average man and woman didn't have time to be that good. There were jobs to do, kids to raise, sheep to shear. If the Pharisees weren't good enough to earn their way into God's kingdom, then nobody was.

Now let me take a quick time-out from our story to ask you a question. If, according to Jesus, the guys who made a living out of being good weren't good enough for heaven, what about you? I've read that story at least a dozen times and here's my conclusion: If Jesus was right, then I am definitely not good enough. I've broken almost all of the Ten Commandments (many times), and I've never once sacrificed an animal for my sins. How about you?

CAN HE DO THAT?

Another thing Jesus did that drove religious leaders nuts was tell people their sins were forgiven. Think about that. The only person who can forgive someone is the one who was offended or wronged. You wouldn't ask me to forgive you for something you did to your mother. You would ask your mother to forgive you. Jesus told people their sins were forgiven when he wasn't even involved in the conflict. Makes no sense.

If that wasn't confusing enough, he reinterpreted Jewish law in such a way as to make it impossible for anybody, even the Pharisees, to keep it.

For example, during his most famous sermon he said, "You have heard that it was said, 'Do not commit adultery.'"

Everybody knew that one. It was one of the Big Ten. But Jesus wasn't content with the common interpretation. He raised the ante:

> "You have heard that it was said, 'Do not commit adultery.' But I tell you that anyone who looks at

a woman lustfully has already committed adultery with her in his heart."

MATTHEW 5:27–28

Now that's not fair, and it's certainly not reasonable. If that's the standard, then, well, we all stand guilty as charged. At least all the men.

Jesus also said:

"You have heard that it was said to the people long ago, 'Do not murder, and anyone who murders will be subject to judgment.' But I tell you that anyone who is angry with his brother will be subject to judgment."

MATTHEW 5:21–22

Claiming to speak for God, Jesus equated anger with murder. Then without batting an eye, he would turn to those who were considered the dregs of society and assure them they had a place reserved for them in heaven. Go figure.

My point? If you are looking for a God who lets good people into heaven, stay away from the New Testament. And by all means avoid the teachings of Jesus. His standards are even higher than those found in the Old Testament law.

Besides, he seems to contradict himself. One minute

he assured bad people they had a place reserved in God's kingdom. Then he turned right around and assured the best people they didn't.

If you think I've misrepresented the teachings of Jesus, check it out for yourself. But first allow me to fast-forward to an incident that may bring clarity to much of what he said.

Chapter 8

BAD GUYS
FINISH FIRST

One particular incident brought eye-popping clarity to what Jesus believed about good people and heaven.

Following his arrest and perfunctory trial, Jesus was beaten and forced to drag his cross toward the place of execution. Luke reports that at some point along the way the Roman guards conscripted a passerby named Simon to carry Jesus' cross for him, the implication being that he was too weak from loss of blood to drag it himself.

Once Jesus was nailed to the cross, Luke records an exchange that took place between Jesus and the men being crucified on either side of him. Before we listen in on their conversation, there are a couple of things about crucifixion you ought to know. In that day, it was considered the most shameful and painful form of execution. A man sentenced to crucifixion was stripped naked before being either tied or nailed to the wooden timbers, and he could hang for days in agony before finally succumbing to death.

Now with that in mind, let's look at what the men crucified beside Jesus said once they recognized who it was that hung between them:

> One of the criminals who hung there hurled insults at him: "Aren't you the Christ? Save your-self and us!"
>
> But the other criminal rebuked him. "Don't you fear God," he said, "since you are under the same sentence? We are punished justly, for we are getting what our deeds deserve. But this man has done nothing wrong."
>
> LUKE 23:39–41

Notice anything about what the second criminal said that is particularly relevant to our discussion? As horrible a death as crucifixion was, the second criminal readily admitted that his life was so horrible that he was actually getting what he deserved. "We are getting what our *deeds* deserve." In other words, "Stack our deeds up and you won't find a good one in there anywhere."

Then the convicted criminal did the unthinkable: He asked Jesus for a favor. He asked Jesus to have mercy on him in spite of his worthless life. He said, "Jesus, remember me when you come into your kingdom" (Luke 23:42).

Keep in mind, this man was in no position to bargain. There was no "from now on," no turning over a new leaf. The opportunity for doing good had come and gone. This was a dead man talking. He had come to the end of his miserable life and there was no chance to make up for lost time. He had lived his life exactly the way he wanted, with no concern for doing the right thing, and now, hours from the end, he suddenly gets religion and asks for mercy.

Now if Jesus, like most people, believed that good people go to heaven and bad people don't, what would you expect him to say to a guy who, by his own admission, had lived a life worthy of such a death?

What would *you* have told him? What if he had raped your sister or murdered your brother? What if you had been maimed for life because of this man's reckless behavior?

None of that mattered to Jesus. Pushing up on the nail that pierced his foot for leverage, he managed to utter these words: "I tell you the truth, today you will be with me in paradise" (Luke 23:43).

Do you realize what that means? It means that Jesus not only didn't believe that good people go to heaven, he believed that bad people *do!* One of his last acts before dying was to promise a criminal a spot in paradise!

Imagine if you had come out to see this man die because of what he had done to you or your family. Imagine how you might have felt as he hung there suffering. Finally, justice is served. Now imagine how irritated you would be to hear this self-proclaimed messiah announce that this filth of a human being would leave this world only to find himself in paradise.

Did Jesus know *nothing* of justice?

Clearly, he did not believe that good people go to heaven.

He was operating off some other premise unknown to this world. It is no wonder many refused to take his teachings seriously. He promised people precisely what they didn't deserve. Whatever God he came to represent, it was not the God worshiped by the majority. It was not the God of the "good people."

JESUS DOESN'T BLEND WELL

The reason I've gone on and on about Jesus is that everyone I have ever met that believes good people go to heaven has good things to say about Jesus. Somehow they are able to blend his teachings and his life with their *good people go* theology. But the two don't really mix.

That's why the religious leaders got rid of him. Jesus was teaching an entirely different message. His contemporaries understood exactly what he was saying. He wasn't offering yet another version of *good guys win.* He was here to establish a new order. So they crucified him. "They" being men who believed with all their hearts that good people—lawkeepers, not lawbreakers—go to heaven.

And yet just about everybody has good things to say about Jesus. Every major cult has adopted parts of his teachings. Even Muhammad, the founder of Islam, had great respect for Jesus—he believed that Jesus was, in fact, a true prophet of God. But Jesus never claimed prophet status. He claimed far more. In fact, he claimed that all the prophets before his time were commissioned to prepare the world for his arrival.

Quite an ego, huh?

Unless, of course, he was right.

But Jesus could not possibly have been right, because his teachings about heaven contradicted everybody else's, before and since.

So if you embrace the notion that good people go to heaven, you can't embrace the teachings or person of Christ. At least, you can't if you are going to be intellectually honest.

I know it feels good to keep Jesus within reach. There *is* something special about him…. But he refuses to be blended with all the other religions which, frankly, are easy to blend. After all, they have a common denominator: Good people make it.

Jesus, on the other hand, said things like, "I am the way and the truth and the life. No one comes to the Father except through me" (John 14:6).

Try blending *that!*

He didn't claim to be *a* way to God—he claimed to be *the* way.

Contrast that with the wisdom of Muhammad:

> Surely those who believe, and those who are Jews, and the Christians, and the Sabians, whoever believes in Allah and the Last day *and does good,* they shall have their reward from their Lord, and there is no fear for them, nor shall they grieve.
>
> THE COW 2.62, ITALICS MINE

Jesus claimed otherwise. Embrace his teachings if you choose, but do so at your own risk. To side with Jesus is to embrace a completely different paradigm from what most world religions are teaching.

If there are many roads to God, as many suggest, Jesus' way is worlds apart from the rest.

RECAPPING

As we come to the close of part 1 of the book, let me summarize what we have said thus far. The *good people go to heaven* view has several seemingly insurmountable problems:

1. We don't know exactly what *good* is. Even our religious leaders can't agree on the subject.
2. Our internal moral gauges aren't much help. They don't line up cross-culturally (or even across the street, for that matter). And as time passes, our definitions of right and wrong tend to change.
3. We have no clear indication from God how the scoring system for good deeds works.
4. It is difficult to reconcile the notion of a good God with a system that is so unclear and seemingly unfair. This is especially true in light of what's at stake.
5. We can't use the Bible as a gauge to measure how close we are to getting in. The Bible doesn't claim to offer a way to heaven through good works. Besides, the catalog of good works listed in the Old Testament is culturally irrelevant and physically impossible to keep.
6. Jesus assured the most religious people of his day that they weren't good enough to enter God's kingdom, while promising criminals and prostitutes that God would gladly welcome them.

Now you may be able to come up with some "What about…?" questions that breathe enough life into the *good people go* view to keep it alive a while longer. But still you are left to wonder and, as time marches on, to worry.

By the way, do you know where the *good people go* view originated? Not with God. It is a view that is as old as creation itself. Ancient men and women believed in multiple gods who, when angry, had to be appeased by their subjects. For millennia, people have been trying to find a successful formula for keeping the gods (or God) mollified and happy. This is a belief that will not go away, despite the fact that it really doesn't make any sense.

But why? Why do we persist in pursuing the favor of a deity who doesn't have the decency to speak clearly? Why do we persist in this charade?

Simple. There are no other good options. Other than abandoning belief in God altogether, there seems to be no other approach.

But all is not as it seems.

There is another way.

PART II

THE ALTERNATIVE

Yes, there is an alternative to the *good people go* view. This is the view I hold, along with almost one-third of the world's population.

According to this view, *forgiven* people go to heaven. And forgiveness is made possible by the sacrificial death of Jesus Christ.

Now before you start rehearsing recycled objections to Christianity, you owe it to yourself to take another look. Why? Because Christianity offers clear and compelling answers to the questions we are left with in the wake of the *good people go* approach to eternity.

Chapter 9

LONG STORY,
SHORT

The primary tenet of Christianity is that a Jewish man named Jesus showed up at the beginning of what is now known as the first century, made some very unique claims, performed any number of miracles, was crucified by the Romans, and came back from the dead three days later. His followers believed he was the promised Messiah—and more. They believed he was the one-of-a-kind Son of God. Borrowing a phrase from his cousin John, they believed Jesus to be the "lamb of God" who came to be sacrificed for the sins of the whole world.

Of course, just because they believed it doesn't make it true. And just because Jesus claimed a unique relationship to God and man doesn't necessarily make his claims true either. But this is undeniably true: He either was or wasn't who he claimed to be.

It should go without saying that Jesus was telling the truth or lying. Either his followers called it as they saw it, or they made up all those stories. But people are hesitant to embrace either of those options. Nearly every major world religion views Jesus as special but not quite as special as he claimed to be. And that in itself is interesting.

When a person claims to be more important than he really is, that generally does not garner support and respect. Yet when it comes to Jesus, everyone is quick to make an exception to the rule. He claimed to be the one-of-a-kind Son of God. On more than one occasion, Jesus equated himself with God. But instead of blowing him off as a lunatic, many continue to quote him in order to gain support for one cause or another.

So what about you? Who do you think Jesus was?

This is an important question, one for which there are only four possible answers. One possibility is that Jesus was lying about himself. I am sure they're out there somewhere, but I've yet to meet anyone who would say, "Jesus Christ was a liar." I don't know why it is so hard for people to say that. If one does not accept Christ's claims about himself, that is really the only view to hold—he was a liar.

A second possibility is that Jesus was crazy—that he truly believed he was God's own son sent here to die for the sins of the world. And because he was so *convinced,* he was *convincing.* We've seen that sort of thing happen before.

A third possibility is that Jesus never claimed to be the Son of God. According to this view, those words were added to the story after he died. This is the safest of all the options. With this view, you can pick and choose what you like from the sayings of Jesus without having to get hung up on whether or not he was the Son of God. It's a really convenient way to think. You can be respectful of Jesus without having to submit to his teachings. After all, he was just a good man with good things to say about a good God.

The final option is that he was exactly who he claimed to be: the Son of God who came to take away the sins of the world.

PICKING OUT BONES

There are problems with all four options. If Jesus was lying or delusional, why would so many continue to follow him after his death? The true Messiah can't *die.* Everybody knows that. His death should have marked the end. Obviously he was either lying or deceived. Besides, he wasn't a very good messiah. Not only didn't he free his nation from Roman rule, he left Israel exactly as he had found her. Why would anyone make up that story about his resurrection? Why keep the dream alive?

Not only did his followers continue to believe in him and spread his teachings, they were all eventually arrested and put to death themselves. No one will knowingly die for a lie. And don't make the mistake of lumping the disciples of Christ in with all the fine individuals who have given their lives for causes through the ages. The followers of Jesus did not die for what they believed—they died for what they claim to have *seen*.

A dead man walking.

Hundreds of thousands of men and women have died for a belief system. Communism, capitalism, Islam, freedom—the list goes on and on. But the first-century followers of Jesus died because they claimed that he came back to life. The resurrection of Jesus was the centerpiece of their message. As one physician, a contemporary of theirs, described it, "With great power the apostles continued to testify to the resurrection of the Lord Jesus."[2]

THE ADDITION CONSPIRACY

While it is tempting and convenient to believe that much was added to the gospels concerning the teachings and deeds of Jesus, this is a terribly complex view to hold and defend. To begin with, you have to come up with a motive.

After Jesus died, it would have been much easier (and less risky) to simply spread his teachings like the disciples of every other religious figure who has come and gone. Jesus was a Jew, as were most of his early followers. Clearly, he wasn't attempting to begin a new religion. In fact, he emphasized and defended the teachings of the Old Testament. Remove his unique claims and all of his miracles from the story, and what you have left is an effort to reform Judaism. There was no need to deify him or claim that he was a miracle worker.

There was no compelling reason to add to what Jesus taught. In fact, his unique claims (purportedly added after his death) make his teaching offensive and difficult to accept. For example, if Jesus never claimed to be the only avenue to God, why would his followers add that when such a statement could discredit everything else he had taught? This is precisely why many in the academic community today refuse to acknowledge that Jesus claimed to be God. They desperately want to hold on to the "acceptable" elements of what he taught, but that nobody-gets-to-the-Father-except-through-me business is problematic. So it is more convenient to believe that he never said it. And that's just my point. Why would anyone add things to what Jesus said if what was added subtracts from the believability of the message? It just doesn't make any sense.

Another problem with believing that someone added to the story is that all four accounts of Jesus' life—the gospels of Matthew, Mark, Luke, and John—were written and disseminated in the region where these unusual occurrences took place at a time when eyewitnesses were still around to dispute their claims. If we had but one account of Jesus' life, that might cast suspicion on the miracle stories and his claims of divinity. However, we have not one, but *four* accounts written by four different individuals. Matthew and John were eyewitnesses. Luke interviewed eyewitnesses.[3] And Mark spent extensive time with Peter, one of Jesus' closest friends.[4]

Is it possible that these four guys got together and made all of this stuff up? Sure. But read the gospels for yourself. Their stories are so different that, clearly, they didn't sit down in a room and compare notes. In fact, no one in the academic community has ever tried to make a case for collusion. Ask any two people who observed the same event to tell you their stories—they will not give identical accounts, although there will be general agreement about what happened with an emphasis on different details. That is exactly what we find in the four gospels.

The Final Option

This brings us to the disturbing notion that perhaps Jesus is exactly who he said he is and that he came for the reason he said he came—to forgive sin. The hitch is that forgiveness, according to Jesus, is not something God can dispense without a sacrifice. So drawing upon a millennium of Jewish law and tradition, Jesus positioned himself as the once-and-for-all sacrifice for sin—the lamb of God.

For more than a thousand years, Jews had been sacrificing animals so that God might overlook their sins. The Old Testament was clear: Sin required death. God had allowed the prescribed death of an animal to temporarily substitute for the death of the sinner. But the death of a lamb did not permanently erase the guilt associated with sin; it merely *atoned* for, or *covered over* the sin.

With this in mind, look again at this exclusionary claim of Jesus: "I am the way and the truth and the life. No one comes to the Father except through me."[5]

How could he claim to be the *only* way to God?

Because he was the lamb of God.

Sin had to be paid for.

He paid.

SOMEBODY'S GOT TO PAY

Needing to make amends for or pay for a wrong deed is not a new concept. Every parent has required a child to "pay" for a sin in some way. Our prisons are full of men and women paying for their sins against society. When you are wronged or taken advantage of, it is natural to want to be paid back for what was done. Our legal system is overrun with cases involving parties who want to be paid back for the damages they incurred at the hands of another.

Strange as it may seem, God requires payment for the injuries *he* has incurred at the hands of mortal man. *Injuries* may not be the best word. I'm not sure how one might injure God. The word *offenses* is probably more appropriate. Each of us is guilty of committing offenses against our creator. The Bible refers to these offenses as sin.

Now if you are offended at being accused of offending God, that's understandable. After all, you are not a bad person and you probably can't think of anything you have done to intentionally offend God. But the Bible says you *have* offended him and that your offense requires payback. And that leaves you in somewhat of a dilemma. You can either toss the Bible aside as an antiquated book of fables, or you can acknowledge that maybe God knows something you don't.

Imagine that. God knowing more than we do. Who does he think he is?

Perhaps you are having difficulty seeing yourself as the kind of person who requires the type of forgiveness that would cost God's son his life. I admit, it does seem rather extreme. But God went to great lengths in the Bible to show just how sinful each of us is and how desperately we all need a savior. Let me illustrate.

BABY STEPS

When Sandra and I had our first child, Andrew, we were convinced that he was perfect. No baby was cuter or smarter than little Andrew. We contacted the folks that publish *Webster's Dictionary* and offered to let them include his picture beside the word *precious* as an illustration. We never heard back.

As Andrew grew, we found it necessary to tell him "no" occasionally. Let me emphasize, *occasionally*. Because he was almost perfect. But once we started saying no, the strangest thing happened: He quit being so precious. There was something inside him we had not seen before, and saying no seemed to bring it out. We said no and something came alive. To our shock and horror we discovered that Andrew had a selfish streak. At times he would rather do what he wanted than what we wanted. We were devastated.

Our rules didn't create his selfish nature. But they sure revealed it. Perhaps if we had never given him boundaries, he would be perfect to this day? Perhaps not. Exercising our parental authority brought out in Andrew what was there all the time—the desire to do things his way, at our expense.

Remember all those Old Testament rules we discussed earlier? I pointed out that the law given by Moses was not intended as a strategy for working our way to heaven, but rather was meant to provide a social and civil framework for the nation of Israel. Well, that was not the only purpose for the law.

The law was also given to make men and women aware of the sin that resided within them. When the nation of Israel was confronted with God's law, they discovered in themselves the same self-centeredness that a simple "no" revealed in Andrew.

The law didn't create sin, but it sure revealed sin. One New Testament author described it this way: "Therefore no one will be declared righteous in his sight by observing the law; rather, through the law we become conscious of sin."[6] Later, he gets rather personal when he writes, "I would not have known what sin was except through the law. For I would not have known what coveting really was if the law had not said, 'Do not covet.'"7

I think I'm a pretty good guy, but if it is against God's law to covet, I'm in trouble. One of my best friends drives a BMW R5 with a touring package to die for. And I want it. I haven't told him that, but in my heart I covet it. When it comes to coveting, I'm guilty every day. But I never knew I was guilty until I knew God required me to be content with what I had.

A NEW FELT NEED

The law makes us painfully aware of our propensity to do things our way at another's expense. And as much trouble as our selfishness gets us into, we continue to bow to it. It chokes the love out of marriages. It drives a wedge between parents and their adolescent kids. It lures men and women outside the boundaries of common sense in the arena of personal finances. It fuels ambition to the point of self-destruction. And after several millennia of human experience, we still have not found a way to rid ourselves of this taskmaster.

What we need is to be, well, saved. We need to be saved, or delivered, from that thing that rages inside us. And we need to be forgiven for all the hurt we have caused as a result of our sin. The problem is, the law convicts me of my sin but does nothing to help me overcome it. The law declares me guilty, but it provides no promise of forgiveness.

Our only hope in the end is to be delivered and forgiven. The law offers provisions for neither. Jesus, on the other hand, came to this earth to be both deliverer and forgiver. No one else in recorded history has ever claimed to be either of those, much less both. The Bible puts it this way:

> For what the law was powerless to do in that it was weakened by the sinful nature, God did by sending his own son in the likeness of sinful man to be a sin offering. And so he condemned sin in sinful man.[8]

We are lawbreakers. We break our own civil laws, and we break God's law. To subscribe to the *good people go* view assumes that we just need to do better. But Christianity teaches that we need a savior.

That is a big, big difference. And it is what divides the Christian faith from every other major world religion.

The reason the Bible doesn't give us a list of behaviors that, if kept, will guarantee us a spot in heaven is because all forty-four authors of Scripture understood that mankind needs a savior, a Messiah, not a to-do list.

Chapter 10

A QUESTION OF
FAIRNESS

I'll be the first to admit that the whole Christianity thing would be much more palatable if it weren't so elitist. *The* way to *the* God through *the* one and only Savior—how can anybody be so dogmatic? As a Christian, I squirm when confronted with the exclusivity of Christ's claims. A lot of Christians do. On the surface the whole thing seems outrageously unfair. But then again, on the surface, the *good people go* view seems so *fair* that it is rarely debated.

In case I lose you during the next few pages, let me go ahead and give you the punch line for the remainder of this book: *Christianity is the fairest possible system in a world that is irreversibly unfair.*

As we will see, it is certainly more fair than a system predicated upon adhering to a list of rules we can't find, created by a God who hasn't had the courtesy to explain the system. But before we broach the question of "Is Christianity fair?" we need to look at the assumption that fuels the fairness debate.

FAIRNESS AND TRUTH

To dismiss Christianity because it is unfair is to assume that something must be fair to be true. Think about it. If, after examining the claims of Christ, you conclude that Jesus could not have been telling the truth because what he says is unfair, then you are using fairness as a test for truth.

For most people, choosing a religion is like choosing a flavor of ice cream—we pick what we like, what we are comfortable with, what suits our taste. That's understandable, but it's not very smart. The issue is not *What do I like?* or *How was I raised?* or *What makes me comfortable?* The issue is *What is true?*

I find that people don't like to be backed into a corner and forced to discuss religion in terms of true versus false. Again, understandable. But once you decide that people live forever *somewhere,* you are staking your eternity on what you choose to believe is true. So it is entirely appropriate to discuss religion in terms of what is and is not true.

Let's face it, something can be absolutely unfair and true at the same time. We don't determine what is true based on whether or not it is fair. While it is *true* that little Susie received a C, it was certainly not fair. And while the umpire's call may have been unfair, it sure enough happened.

Obvious as that may be, I have talked to dozens of people who flippantly cast aside the claims of Christ because they are deemed unfair. These people express their opinions in a variety of ways, but essentially what they are saying is, "Christianity is unfair; therefore, I don't believe it is true." If at the end of this book you are not convinced that Christianity is *fair,* it still says nothing about whether or not Christianity is *true.* Fairness does not determine truth.

Cuts Both Ways

In fairness, let me be quick to point out that just because the *good people go* system isn't fair, that doesn't mean it isn't true. But there is one big difference. The initial appeal of the *good people go* view is that on the surface it appears to be perfectly fair. But as it turns out, it is not fair at all!

Is it true? You must decide that for yourself. The problem is, there are a dozen variations on the theme. There's the Islamic version, the Mormon version, the Hindu version, the Orthodox Jewish version, and the list goes on. Each claims to have *the* correct list of things you must do to please God. And each claims to follow *the* prophet(s) who received his teachings directly from God.

Christianity is different. The initial appeal is not fairness, but forgiveness. In fact, as we will see, Christianity is based on the premise that God laid aside fairness and opted for mercy and grace instead.

PLAYING THE FAIRNESS CARD

Life is not fair. Life will never be fair. Life can't be fair.

I am not convinced that any of us is really as concerned as we pretend to be about any of these statements. When people complain about something not being fair, it is almost always a smoke screen for the fact that they are not getting something they want. Most of us walk around pretending to be the fairness police when, in fact, we usually play the fairness card when we are the ones being treated "unfairly."

Every parent knows this to be the case. When have you known a child to throw down the fairness gauntlet when he got more than his fair share of something? I never expect to hear the following at my house:

"No fair! My piece is bigger."

"No fair! I got more presents than everyone else."

"No fair! I got to sit in the front seat last time."

A couple of nights ago, I was sitting behind the backstop, watching my oldest son, Andrew, pitch. The count was full, three balls and two strikes. Andrew wound up and threw a fastball about four inches off the outside corner of the plate. I dropped my head, thinking he had just walked the batter. To my surprise, I heard the umpire shout, "Strike!"

What do you suppose I did? I sat right there and whispered, "Thank you, Lord." I didn't have the slightest inkling to jump up, grab the backstop, and inform the umpire of what a lousy call he had made. I didn't demand fairness in this situation. I was content with mercy. Now as you might expect, the father of the batter felt differently. And you know what? If Andrew had been at bat and that happened to him, I would have felt the same way. Strange how that works.

We rarely expend much emotion demanding fairness when we get more than we deserve. I say "rarely" because there are times when we are willing to come to the defense of others who are being treated unjustly. At times, we are even willing to sacrifice our own time or money for the sake of those who didn't get their fair share. But most of the time, we are content to simply feel concern for people in those situations. The fact that I have more than my fair share doesn't bother me to the point of redistributing my wealth among those who don't. A few dollars here and there, maybe. But redistributing to the point of putting everybody on a level economic playing field? Not me.

RETHINKING OUR DEMANDS

Despite the fact that we are fickle in our demands for justice, we sure find it easy to demand fairness from God. But that's only because of our distorted application of fairness. The truth is, if you were to sit down and evaluate your divine demands, I think you would conclude, as I have, that you don't really want God to be fair. A truly fair God would give you exactly what you deserve and nothing more.

Do you *really* want God to give you what you deserve?

If you believe that only good people go to heaven, the only honest answer to that question is "I don't know." Why? Because none of us knows what we deserve; we can't find the standard by which we are being measured.

This is where Christianity really stands apart from

the pack. The God of Christianity never claims to be fair. He goes *beyond* fair. The Bible teaches that he decided *not* to give us what we deserve—that's *mercy*. In addition, God decided to give us exactly what we don't deserve—we call that *grace*.

Is Christianity fair? Absolutely not. But if you take the Bible seriously, the last thing you would want is for God to be fair.

He tried being fair once. Things didn't work out very well.

THE DAY FAIRNESS DIED

Once upon a time, life was fair. It didn't last very long, but there was a time when all things were equal. Everybody on earth had an equal opportunity to access and discover the truth about God. Everybody on earth knew exactly what God's standard was. Everybody understood the rules and the consequences for breaking them. Everybody had meaningful employment, a place to live, a healthy family environment. Things were perfect. Life was simple. Instead of ten commandments, God issued only one. One commandment. He didn't bother to etch it on a tablet of stone. Everybody committed it to memory.

The time I am referring to is recorded for us in the book of Genesis. The Garden of Eden was a perfect environment created by a perfect God for his prize creations. For reasons we won't go into here, God chose to give mankind a gift that could be used for unimaginable good or evil—the gift of freedom. Specifically, the freedom to choose.

And for choice to have meaning, God gave Adam and Eve options: Obey this one rule or disobey it. Obedience signified their recognition of and gratitude to God, creator and provider. Disobedience would result in death.

What happened next is of extreme importance. I realize the entire Garden of Eden story may be nothing more to you than an ancient attempt to explain the origins of mankind. But bear with me a moment while I attempt to explain why Christians believe it to be far more. For herein lies the answer to a question that has plagued you since you were old enough to think for yourself—a question that has no answer apart from this ancient piece of human history.

When Adam and Eve ate of the forbidden fruit, they—not God—introduced sin and all its consequences into their fair, just, and perfect world. In that moment, the possibility for fairness came to an end. From that day forward, men, women, and children have treated one another unfairly. God had two choices: Start over, or resort to mercy and grace.

So next time you are frustrated with God over the injustices in the world—or in *your* world—remember, Christianity offers an explanation. We believe that the current system was not the original system. It is a distortion of what God intended. God's original design was exactly what you might wish for: It was fair. Everybody was on a level playing field. Everyone had an equal opportunity to believe and behave. But just when God had everything the way he wanted it, Adam and Eve exercised their right to choose. And they chose poorly.

Unfair, isn't it? If the Bible is true, we pay every day for a decision made by two naked ancestors we never met who lived in a garden we aren't even sure existed. Why should *we* pay for *their* sins?

I don't know. But we do.

Chances are, at some time in your life you have suffered as a result of someone else's choices. It wasn't fair. But it happened. And there are probably people wandering around this planet who were hurt by decisions you made; they did nothing to deserve the resulting pain or loss, but their lives were forever impacted.

Sandra and I have a friend who works two jobs to support her little girl while her deadbeat ex-husband gallivants around with his girlfriends in his new car. It wasn't Nancy's fault that her husband decided to fool around on her, but she's sure paying a price for it.

So yes, I believe that we have all been taken down a notch or two by a couple of folks we never met. Do I think it is fair? Nope. But I believe it is true. And it is an experience that has been repeated among men and women ever since.

FAIR TO WHOM?

To put all of this in perspective, I believe that God suffered as well the day fairness died. In order to untangle us from the web we had spun for ourselves, he had to do something very unfair. He had to send his son to this earth to die for sins he didn't commit.

Is Christianity fair? It is certainly not fair to God. Christians believe that God sent his son to die for *your* sins and *mine*. Fairness would demand that we die for our own sins. But the good news is that God opted for grace and mercy over fairness.

I don't know how you explain the evil and unfairness in the world. I don't know how you account for bad things happening to good people. Christianity offers both an explanation and a solution. The explanation is that when sin entered the world, life became irreversibly unfair. The solution is…well, the solution is the topic of our final chapter.

Chapter 11

THE FAIREST OF
THEM ALL

When my children were very young, I bought a used Infiniti. It was the nicest car I had ever owned. It was in mint condition, and I intended to keep it that way. Unfortunately, I was alone in my pursuit.

One Saturday morning, as I was taking out the trash, I noticed something on the hood of my car. I walked over for a closer look and to my utter dismay discovered that someone had scratched the letter *A* into the paint. Beside the *A* were attempts at several other letters.

I was furious. Within seconds my two sons were standing beside me as I demanded to know who scratched up my car. For a moment there was silence.

Then Garrett, who was five at the time, piped up: "Allie did it."

Allie, my youngest child and only daughter, was a whopping three and a half years old. I called her out to the garage, pointed to my hood, and said, "Allie, did you do that?"

She sheepishly looked up at me and said, "Yes, sir, Daddy."

OPTIONS

What was I going to do? There was no way in the world for me to explain to Allie the significance of what she had done and what it was going to cost me in dollars, time, and hassle to get it fixed. There was no point in telling her that now I was going to have to take the car to the shop, rent a car, and pay for the rental car as well as the repair. She had no context for understanding any of that.

It would have been equally absurd to demand that Allie pay for the damage. Fair, maybe, but unrealistic. What does two or three hundred dollars mean to a three-year-old? The numbers wouldn't even register. And where would she get the money?

So what do you do in that kind of situation? Sever the relationship? Demand payment? Rant and rave? Of course not.

I did the only thing I could do for someone I loved

as much as I loved her. I knelt down and said, "Allie, please don't do that anymore."

She said, "Yes, sir, Daddy." Then she hugged me and went back inside.

I continued to love her as much as ever. And I paid for the damage she caused. I wasn't concerned about fairness. It wasn't appropriate to figure out what was fair. What was most appropriate was grace and mercy. Even if it meant that I had to pay for what she had done.

PAYBACK

God sees your sin as a debt you can't pay. There's no point in asking you to. To think that being good will somehow make you square with God would be like Allie promising to clean up her room after being confronted with the damage she had done to my car. Cleaning up her room doesn't pay me back. It's a nice gesture, but it doesn't fix my car.

Christianity teaches that when man sinned, God opted for forgiveness rather than fairness. He opted for grace and mercy rather than justice. What he offers you is more than fair. A New Testament writer explained it this way: "You see, at just the right time, when we were still powerless, Christ died for the ungodly."9

"Powerless" means we could not do anything about our condition—we were without hope unless somebody intervened on our behalf. The reason good people don't go to heaven is that there *aren't* any good people. There are only sinners. Granted, some aren't quite as bad as others. But from God's perspective, everybody has carved a few letters into the hood of the car and can't pay for the damage. We can all promise to do better, and some of us may even scurry upstairs to clean our rooms. But none of us can pay God back.

The Bible goes on to say, "But God demonstrates his own love for us in this: While we were still sinners, Christ died for us."[10]

In other words, while we were treating God and others unfairly, God decided to forgive us and pay for our sins himself. While we abandoned what was fair, God went beyond fair and paid for our sins.

Good people don't go to heaven. *Forgiven* people go to heaven.

WHAT COULD BE MORE FAIR?

Is Christianity fair? You'll have to decide that for yourself. I've come to the conclusion that it is beyond fair. What could be fairer than this?

- Everybody is welcome.
- Everybody gets in the same way.
- Everybody can meet the requirement.

All three of these statements are supported by one of the most often quoted verses in the New Testament:

> "For God so loved the world that he gave his one and only Son, that whoever believes in him shall not perish but have eternal life."[11]

"Whoever" includes everyone who is willing. Believing in him is the only requirement. Believing means placing one's trust in the fact that Jesus is who he claimed to be and that his death accomplished what he claimed it accomplished.

THE LAST HURDLE

The ultimate question each of us must answer for ourselves is not whether Christianity is fair. The more important question is "Is Jesus who he claimed to be?" In other words, "Is Christianity true?"

If after reading this book you are convinced it is not, then you are certainly to be commended for your willingness to investigate the Christian faith in spite of your reservations. If you are still not sure, I hope you will continue to investigate. But if, during our brief time together, a light came on for you, I want to encourage you to do something to mark this moment.

Would you say a simple prayer expressing your gratitude to God for sending his son to be your personal savior?

Saying a prayer won't make you a Christian. Placing your faith in Christ as your savior makes you a Christian. Prayer is just a way of expressing to God that you have come to the conclusion that Jesus is in fact his son and your savior.

The following is a sample prayer. You can ignore it or repeat it verbatim. What matters is that you believe Jesus is who he claimed to be and that you are no longer trusting in what you have done, or will do, to get you to heaven.

Heavenly Father, thank You for not being fair.
Thank You for instead being merciful.
I believe true fairness would have separated
me from You forever, because that's what I deserve. Thank
You for sending Jesus to die for my sins.
I now place my faith in him as my savior.
Thank You for sending him to die in my place.

The word *gospel* means "good news." The good news is that good people don't go to heaven—forgiven people do.

And if you have placed your faith in Jesus Christ as your savior, you are one of those forgiven people!

If you prayed this prayer for the first time after reading this book and would like some information about next steps, please visit our website at www.howgoodisgoodenough.com.

NOTES

1. Quoted in H. A. Evan Hopkins, "Christianity—Supreme and Unique," *The Inadequacy of Non-Christian Religion: A Symposium* (London: Inter-Varsity Fellowship of Evangelical Unions, 1944), 67.

2. Acts 4:33.

3. Luke 1:1–4.

4. 1 Peter 5:13.

5. John 14:6.

6. Romans 3:20.

7. Romans 7:7.

8. Romans 8:3.

9. Romans 5:6.

10. Romans 5:8.

11. John 3:16.

ABOUT THE AUTHOR

Andy Stanley is an author and speaker from Atlanta, Georgia. He is the author of the 1998 *Foreword* Book of the Year finalist *Visioneering,* as well as *Choosing to Cheat* and *The Next Generation Leader.* Andy and his wife, Sandra, have two sons and a daughter.